*Shadow Breathing*

# *Shadow Breathing*

Julie Flanders

*Shadow Breathing*

© 2018 Julie Flanders
ISBN: 978-0-9886456-3-9
Printed in the USA

*For Rooney & Bud*

# Contents

*Acknowledgments*

Edited by Emil Adler & Marina Belica
Cover by Mick Wieland Design

Special thanks to:
OP(iii), LLC
Munroe Hill Press
Calcaterra Photography
Yale University

## *Angels on a Pin*

You shed blessings
Like ash from the palm of a great saint
These gifts of you fall
To join the earth
I fell from you too
Gravity ready to grab me from you
Into a scream-song
Finite enough to be beautiful

The beauty of always
Is too much to appreciate
We find our voices raised to smaller gods
Singing songs that fit the odds
Of our own bounded equations

When we think of all that
Dark matter tugging on the light
Or that explosion so terrible and bright—
Our burning birth—
We fight for all we are worth
From doubt and trust
We raise a stardust fist, and shout
I exist

As the universe expands
It's getting faster—

To shed its history—
So we will lose this past
Or see it crawl away
As the edges of what we can see
Slip from us and leave no trace

Do you believe that?
Is that a fact?
Will we accelerate toward nothing
Or will we contract
Until the whole experiment collapses
Relapses
Falls back into itself
Each star a dark and fatal trap
Subsuming light

I do not believe in everlasting night
Or even one long, dark corridor
Leading nowhere
But you are not here to help me
Prove anything anymore

And yet you are everywhere
I see you are all around
And inside of me
You shed blessings from the trees
You sing with this year's just-born birds
And you pray on monks' knees

I am always thinking of the hive
And the millions of bees
That excavate the flowers
For their filthy and intoxicating nectar
In order to return to it
In a hum of desire
In a scrumptious, buzzing vector of delight
To the queen who sits in some deep interior
Forgoing the pleasures of flight
To conjure honey

The world is complete
You soak yourself in pollen
Until your whole body is sweet

I saw you transform
I saw you change shape
I saw you leave this painful illusion
And make a great escape

I do not know if you were ready
I do not know if there was a choice
Between eternal darkness and eternal sun
I do not know how much you have never begun
Or finished
And what I do know, I am forgetting

But I take comfort in the world

You have left me

Where you shed blessings

Like skin

And as the whole world ends

We begin again

## Even Before Eden

Somewhere in the corner of language

Where the first sounds

Changed by a fire

Sent smoke toward the caves

Gave teeth, tongue and song to human desire

Rising up and slamming down

In a dance of feet, legs, hands

Clapping secrets

Feeling the thrum and beat of meanings

That surge through us

Like some empyrean directive

Eyes open to the sky we still gaze at

Each a detective into the past

Staring into the dark glass of the sky

And the lattice of stars

And all the mysterious architecture of Chaos

And Theos

We bring through us

As we chatter words

Chew through the symbols of the day

In a casual, irritating way

Spinning stories of sin and magic

Weaving the webs of strange and tragic heroes

Creating the duality of ones and zeros

By which we live and interconnect

By which we attempt to become whole

Even as we dissect our experience

And use these words

Husked of their history

Divorced from the hair and blood

Of human and divine mystery

Sentences forming paragraphs

Quotation marks and commas

Obscuring the powerful, terrible grammar

From which we sprang

When we first sounded out the name of god

As the heavens sounded the world into shapes

Just odd enough for us to live in

Filling all the corners of the earth

Forgiving nothing with our tongues

Forgetting the birth of these dark songs

Forgetting they were ever sung

As the world slips unnoticed from our lips

And we separate from ourselves

From the rich Vedic wells of language

And connection

Past, through, and beyond detection

We carry secrets no vivisection can reveal

And this is the secret that our words conceal—


Words serve

To make imagination real

## On Three

We hurl ourselves into the maverick
Rising with its own fierce currency
You wonder if we'll make it back from this
I never wonder anything

Your mother lay there on the bed
So drunk
We both thought she was dead
But she was just pulling the morning up
Over her head
Like a blanket over a child

You curl your lip
Your laugh is wild
Her hair grows out in a magnificent pile
Almost like a crown of thorns

We blow the morning
Watch the storms exploding
Until the world reforms itself
And us

The greater world begins
Out where the curtain is
You have to look beyond the crowd
Of surfaces

You wonder if the world is your audience
I just notice everyone applauding us

Your brother never made it back
From Afghanistan
You told me
That's how the world makes a boy into a man
Who am I to disagree
I'm just the one you're telling it to
I'm just me
Being secretly glad it was him and not you

Some things you don't say
Even if they're true

Your mother's crying in her sleep
A secret you're determined to keep from everyone
But me

Let's go
Hold hands and jump the cliff
The water will catch us
Like some tiny gift
And toss us around in a froth of waves
We'll be like toys
That the ocean saves for itself
Saved for another day

I don't know what else to say

I don't even know what else to do

Except to jump out with a scream

And swim into the water

With you

All the way in

No fear

No doubt


All the way in

Is the only way out

## Under Tucson Skies

Cacti standing with their noses in the air
Dreaming of arms
They will have one day
A century from now
One among them does a sun salutation
Like some ancient yoga instructor
Ineluctably praising the source of all creation
Arms rising in permanent elation

I miss you here
Where each tiny patch of green
Is the fiercest miracle I have ever seen
Where the desert and the chapped mountains
Make me appreciate the thoughtless fountains of Manhattan
And the soft, color-bent satin of flowers
In the classic garden where I sit with you
And stare out at the square foothill towers of Fifth Avenue

Yesterday I saw a small yellow bloom growing
Amid the vicious scrub of weeds that spread
On this loom of desert
Where I could believe that nothing grows
And yet this tiny flower was as thrilling as any rose

My thoughts of you today are like thoughts of the sea
Spilling limitless beauty and power

Far away from me

And as I sit and marvel at these desert skies

As blue as the ocean of your eyes


I remember that once, long ago

There was water here

Deep enough to fill the canyons

The cactus still remembers that

And reaches down where the earth is dry

To pull its water toward the sky

Each limb a green and pink

And breathing fountain


And then I think of you again

And see the mountain

## Waiting on Park for the 66


The walls are cracking

In your parents' house

They no longer repair things

The ceiling in the kitchen has a hole

That leads into some darkness

Above

The bathroom door is broken

And the whole house frowns

In need of some younger love


Decades ago

I would call you there

In that house

On a dial phone

From my own ramshackle house

Where I felt so alone

In the place I used to call home

Where things fell down a lot sooner

In my world than in yours

Where you were still just a boy

And I was still just a girl


And we laughed

As if there was nothing wrong

As if my mother was not cracking up

Like the walls around her

We just laughed
And that was our form of repair
You just met me
In the place between here
And there

Last year
We renovated our own home
And as we excavated
Books, papers, letters, noise
We tried to say goodbye
To everything we own
To decades of love and life
And old toys
Loss and pain
And all the decorations of memory
And we began to poise
At the edge of a new nest
Worried to see our boy fly
Away, knowing
It happens in its own time
Not yours and mine

The other day
You told me how as a baby
You would dance
And shake and rock
To American Bandstand playing

Rock Around the Clock
Something you don't remember
But your parents do
Something I wish I had been around
To actually see you do

Looking back
And looking forward
I can feel us moving away
And feel us moving toward
What is foreign
And familiar

Our son
Looking up at his own sky
Looking back at his old home
Where you and I
Push against the tides of rot
And despair
And remind ourselves only
To care
And to care

Remember
When he was young
And he would have a scary nosebleed
I thought it was the end of the world
And you would laugh at me

And stop the flood

Telling stories of your own nose

To his nose

Blood to blood

Where we all bleed together


I know

Houses cannot be built to stand

Forever

But sometimes when we visit

Your parents' house

I want to hold your hand

I want to fix the ceiling

And the door

I want to turn the clocks back

And restore the old dial phone


Most of all, I suppose

I want to give them back a home

I want them to know in their hearts

That we are their family

And they are not alone

# *I.N.R.I.*

You carved your initials into the wooden pew
That held our heads bowed
Your wicked face in front of you
My knees tucked under my short skirt
You stared at my thighs
Aggression or flirt
You moved your sharp scissors
Into the wood
Leaving raw fissures
As the priest droned on
In what must have been a prayer

I could smell your teenage attitude
In the thick, church air
Layered with the residue of incense there
And I still cannot forget
Your lank, stringy hair
Or the way your lips were dry
But your mouth was wet
As you leaned in for a strange bite
Or kiss
And I let you
Even though you actually missed my mouth
And kiss-bit my chin
Landing a little bit south of my lips
As you tried to get your tongue in

I am still embarrassed

I can feel my stomach lurch

To think of you

Even now

As I come back to that same church

And kneel there decades later

By myself

Right there

Where you knelt beside me

In a secret never shared with anyone else

I wince at the thought of your old nickname

And burn with a residual, ridiculous shame

After all, you are not even alive

But your initials, carved there, still survive

In the scar

# Man Overboard

All the woe-begotten, joy-besotted
Debutantes
Wait for him
For what he wants
When he wants it

She is not about to find him
In the archives
Where the history of the world
Hides behind him
And the women who could never
Possess or unwind him
Make a play to be what defines him

They are not of consequence

All the faith-forsaken, overtaken
Hypocrites
Wait for him
Where the future sits
In its bits and pieces

She is keen to see what time
Releases
From the dungeons
Where the history of a man

Comes and bludgeons

Him

And the visions that could never

Cast him asunder

Make a play to be what becomes under–

Stood

The way she wishes it would


The way it never could

Once

It had been done

# *Pang*

We live in staccato continuities
Ignoring the space between the infinities
That rest between the stagger of pulses
Moving to please
Feigning choreographies
Ignoring how ill at ease we are in our biologies
With the spasms of uncertainties
That rule our timed signatures
And mark the keys in which we sing

Are we creatures of meaning
Or sense, creatures even of anything
Or random beings, chance atoms
In collisions of seeming meaning
Dancers
In a vision of divine intelligence

I don't understand any of what you have said
He smiled, how could you, and shook his head

I wonder if there is anything better
Than spinning around on the beach
Arms spread
As wide as you can reach
Turning your body round and round
And round

Until you fling what is left of you
Onto the sand-dusted ground
Allowing the spin to continue its illusion
As you lie still
In the body-mind confusion
Of memory

I remember him that way
As a strong sensation—
Like the smell of lilacs on a spring day
Like the salt and dead sea creatures
That scent the ocean's rich spray—
Of frustration
With no way to convey what he meant

Are we earth-borne
Or heaven-sent
Is there sin in every thought
Should we repent for being who we are
And how and why
Did the whole conversation start
Was it ever really
One dense star-exploding blast
One sneeze of cosmic ever-ness
That could not last
One everlasting flash
From which we all sprang
Into this illusion

He spoke his effusions
And I sang

And when the bells tolled
He was the one for whom they rang
A rich and unforgettable staccato

Pang-pang-pang-pang

## Fly Back

The hawk sees differently
Its eye finds no horizon
It does not fear falling
It feels life calling it into the sky
And opens its body up
To fling itself into empty space
And to make circles
With the traces of its silhouette

Grief is what you can't remember
Grief is what you can't forget

A painted pinecone
From some September classroom
Where you asked for a glass of water
But the teacher told you to sit down
And the class stared at you
And that one girl turned around
To say you were a joke

Grief is white smoke rising from a cold fire

There is no cure
There is no place to go
To inquire about how to make it stop

Grief is an eternally spinning top
Like the one on that boy's desk
When the principal came
And called out your name

Grief feels like you are under arrest
Like you are in chains
And about to be taken away
Like there's a secret the room knows about you
But no one will say

Grief is the moment you can't turn away
You can't have a glass of water

You are thirsty
You are drowning
You are the only daughter of a thousand dying suns
About to expire, but not yet
Not until they scorch what you are seeing
Eclipse your way of being
Into a blur

Grief arrives
But doesn't leave
It just occurs

Grief changes who you were
Into who you will never be again

Grief is a prayer without an amen
Grief stuns you with its fierce beauty

And so you rise from your chair
Reluctant with duty
And you go to the door
Where the principal waits
To tell you what no one anticipates

Stop the world
Stop all the pretending
This is where life begins
This is the true ending
Where the hero dies
And his daughter is left thirsty
Holding a piece of pink chalk
Can't cry, can't breathe
Can't walk

One day we look up and see a hawk flying
A dark shape
In stark relief against a white sky

We are all the circles we draw
With our life
We are all the courage we have
To say goodbye

Grief is when we circle back

With no horizons

But those we hold inside


We feel the call of life

To fly

So we open our wings

And fling our bodies into space

Until we rise

## Elsewhere

I can not remember the word you gave me
It must be there somewhere
Right next to the keys I left in Montreal
Or the box of chocolates
There on the stone wall
Shaped like a heart, fire engine red
You never saw it
Because you too were somewhere else
Instead

So many times
We miss what we had expected
The word blurts
Rejection
And we feel its sting until it hurts

Some women tell me it's all in the mind
All suffering
Just something you have defined
Some kind of meaning you give to events
As you keep screening the horizon
For sense
For a happiness you believe never relents
But is always there
Elsewhere

You find no up
You find no down
There is no direction
To be found
Wanting

And yet you circle around
Trying to avoid danger
Trying to find your way to the crest
Of a mountain range
Where the air is brittle
And you can feel the wind-knife
Whittle your face
Lifelike

Tragedy is a midwife to this confusing place
Where we are born into mystery and desire
Born where we can't even form a word
For what might inspire us to grace

And so we fall on our faces
And so we cry in secret places
And so we search for where the escape is
Hiding
From the feeling we have
When we try to change shape
When we want to die

I lost that word
And not because I didn't try

But if you still love me
And sometimes I don't remember why
You continue to remind me
Of something I cannot deny

A touch is enough

## *Kindling*

Lost poems all over my life
Strewn across abandoned floors
Slipped under closed doors

I have scribbled my heart on my sleeves
On napkins
On the backs of dead leaves
I have burned love in a pyre of shame
Set fire to the words that cradled your name
And watched what was left of you
Rise
In flames

For all I've lost
Looks, life
Humor, sleep
There is still a part of you
I secretly keep on scraps of paper
Buried deep in journals I never read
You survive where I have bled
And bleed
You are still alive
Somewhere

Somewhere
You are not dead

I wish I had the lost words of you

I once regretted

Poems I have unwed

And let pass through me

The part of you I hated

Then


Now

Finally

I've come to love again

I've come to know you are the lost one

I tried to lose


And you are the last one

I would ever choose

To forget

## The Sovereign Ghost

You could bemoan the loss of stature
The way the whole World's Fair fell
Into disrepair
Though skeletons still stand there
And ghosts permeate the urban air
Where once there were amusement parks
Now there are only dark sparks of the past
Near the highway
Where future ghosts speed past
What cannot be measured
By an autocrat

We do not need a sublime ruler
Of inches
A fool who never quite found his footing
To animate the husk of a world
Shrugged off by unseen shoulders
Yet still standing in awe of itself

We are riding the Ferris Wheel
Of changes that seem to matter
We are flying through landscapes
That would delight the Mad Hatter
And invite Alice to forego tea
In favor of worlds that collide
More spectacularly

The world that has yet to happen
Inside of me

Reminds me of you
A place I used to be able to imagine
Perfectly
Now lingers in the tingle-tangle of nostalgia
And the fading details of a picture
On a strange angle
Once clear
Now distant
And blurry with other people's tears

I promise you that whatever I forget
I will make up for
Penitent and in emotional arrears
With something I invent
That appears to represent all the ways you were
Important

You still are
Everything you never were, but wished to be
And I still am in awe
Of the world inside of me
Where you reign
From clouds of history

## *Internal Portico*
(for S.P.L.)


The world could bowl you over

Or you could simply roll

With the sunlight

Into the edges of the day

As the world falls over itself

Into tomorrow


Sorrow is a terrible sweetness

That cannot be swallowed into the body

As if you were too full

Or as if you were hollow

Or as if you were sinking

With the sun

As it moves over the brink

Past the view of your portico

Into a darkness that cannot be spun

Into galaxies you recognize


The stories you were told as a boy

Were lies

But you miss your father

Who was warm and wise

And strong

Who gave you a place to go

And to belong

Sometimes you wish you could return
To that time
And a part of you tries
When suddenly the world opens again
In your own child's eyes

Remember when you spoke in tongues
Ran fields
Until the air burned in your lungs

You still speak the body-english of those days
When you move or jump
And land
Or when you create a new phrase with your son
Or when the light comes up over the water
And you take your daughter's hand

Love and sorrow are beautiful twins
Where life is ending
And life begins

The world does bowl you over
And you could simply fall to the side
Or you could roll back to us now
Where life is short
And deep
And wide

## Cocoon

Whatever crawled up and died
Inside you
Became who you are
Your heart bounded by a thick scar
Your face shaped like a smile
With saw-like teeth
While everything you hold back
Is creased by that half-wreath of skin
Your eyes blink
And you hold the creature in

But I hear your real voice
Smothered within
I hear you crying an old familiar song
Below the level of hearing
Far deeper than your false sense of right or wrong
I still hear you and I know
That you belong right where you are

Long ago, I cried
When I thought the monster ate you
When I saw the hatred rise up in your light eyes
I remember you then
And yet you became a creature
I could not recognize

Now I know
You are the sweet remnant of yourself
Trapped beneath a fallen skein
Like something precious on a bottom shelf
Behind years of mess and collected junk
Hidden like a secret thing
Like a diamond ring
On a ship that has sunk
In the middle of the sea

But I dive down
And I know you hear me
I am singing your old familiar song
The one you'll remember
The one that means you still belong to me

I am calling you
To hear your own voice
The one you had when you were young
To let the ocean in
To drown the silence
To fill your lungs
And make whatever ocean sound
Will move across your tongue

I will help you rise up
Out of yourself
I will help you return to me

I will find you on the shelf
Where you believe you are
Dead, stale, rotten

I see you there
I have not forgotten

Whatever crawled up inside you
And seemed to die
Was a caterpillar then
And it doesn't matter why
Just let it come
Just let it become
Something else

Let it become the butterfly

## Some Point Called Center

If they came
As cascading as arpeggios
As parachutes out of the sky
Would you look away
Thinking of angels
Thinking of butterflies

Or would you think
Of lemmings on the brink of a century
Of a whole dirty-faced people
Still stomping the ground
Like human shakers
In hopes of rain
In the dust bowls of a country
Crazy
In praise of the rainmakers

For there were men who
Once upon a time
Could conjure water from the skies
Could bring down waves of
And days of water
Right there before your eyes
Washing clean a wave of crime
Even before it starts

Did you mean to say that water is rising

As it parts

Or did you mean that some men

Could bring what others could not hope to ask for

In their hearts


I hear a hum, a sound

Right now

As an airplane moves overhead

A roar, a growl

And I remember

I am not a creature of the night sky

And its dark cowl

I am first of all

A creature of the sky-fall


I am an owl

I am the dust that lands

And settles where it is foul

Where it is rotting

And growing

Like mold on a wet towel


I am the consonant sound of life

I am the vowel

Of the big-banging universe

Expanding in a cosmic howl

I am afraid of its terrifying openness
I need to feel the gravity
Of some point called center
Pulling me back onto my feet
To feel the heaviness of me
On this earth
Somehow present
Somehow complete

Like stars and sand
I know that I am standing out
And standing in
For time

I am standing in a strange rhyme
Of elements that thrill millions
Not lifted up against my will
Still walking there
Talking, breathing
I take this air in
And let my voice trill nonsense
I am this atmosphere
I bring it into me
Until I am ready for the dare

I breathe life into the ancient air
It mixes with me
It is always there

It is as full of me as I am
Full of it

And I am full of all its repercussions
And the molecules of Russians
Who ruled an empire with their breath
And now in my life
I think of their death
And how their molecules of air are mine
To breathe

And I have so many words I love
To design
And to cut with the knife of my mind
Into the cloth of worlds falling apart
Or coming together
With myself in them
I wrap myself in those worlds
And in these words
I am in

We are such sad machines
Or such happy creatures
Are we birds or music
Are we somehow major or minor thirds
Or chords and melodies
Spinning around

When we are making sound
Are we making ourselves up
Or writing ourselves down

Are we an urge of butterflies
An arpeggio of angels
Or a cloud of soldiers
Parachuting out of the skies
Into a field we will not storm together
Where the climate has already changed
The weather

Are we the creatures that wait
For a promise
That will one day resurrect us
From all the loss we have caused
As if we didn't know it would affect us
Killing the caterpillar
For its wings
Weathering the consequences
Transformation brings

We are straining now
To break the silk that binds us
So we can fly
Or fall into the milk
Of human kindness

## Black Box

There was no black box
With your voice
To tell me how it happened
You were just gone

And with you
So many stories vanish
To a horizon
Past anything I can see

I wish I had your ending
Here to guide me
To lead me to understand how
You handed me the world
In front of me
And now
I no longer have your hand
To hold

When I was young
I you took my freezing fingers
In your big palm
Which was full of some kind of sunshine
That made me calm
And incredibly warm

If I had all the information
How would that inform me
Any better than I already am
How would knowing how
Change what happened
Into something I can understand

One time in a huge snowstorm
You helped me build a fort
And I pretended I was an ice princess
And that small cave was my court

Back on that wildwood terrace
You were my king
Our servants drank cocoa
And ate Cracker Jacks
And I wore the Cracker Jacks ring
Like something royal

That ring was worth everything
In our kingdom

The world crashes
A million times a day
And a million other people wonder
Maybe in the same way
How did my beloved slip away

If there were a black box

Where you had said goodbye

Would I be any less afraid to fly

After you


And when you took your last look

At the sky

Did you have a hand to hold

As kind

As warm

As your own


That is what I will imagine now

And pretend

It is what I have always known

## The Dead Queen in the Rose Chamber

You whisper-listed your interest
As if it were some top secret illustration
Meant only for my eyes
Signaled by your eyebrows
Right there with all those highbrows around us
Spouting so much information it could drown us

You told me you were the lone jerk
In a sea of conformists
I told you I was the type to do my homework
And then show it to the kid in the seat next to me
Subversive codependent–cheat
I'm always looking for the rules to break
Inside the rules I keep

You probably thought I meant it
You probably thought that neither of us could prevent it
But you were not seeing the kind of cruel and dispassionate
Kind of human I was being

You see it wasn't my first time at that table
It wasn't the first time I would play Cain
To someone's Abel
I knew that one day I would open your throat
Not because I hated you
But because I loved you

Because you swam across the moat
To rescue what you thought was me

Obviously we see what we want to see

I saw you—All frog and prince
I saw you doing your best to convince me
And everyone else of your innocence
I knew you were guilty before we even started
I knew what was black in your soul
Before I knew what was in your heart
And I decided to be prepared
To look back at you as you stared at me
And pretend that yes, this is going to happen
This is going to happen
As happiness sometimes does
I told you silently that you could count on this
(What might be)

And now you can remember
What it was you thought was really me
You can remember the kiss
You can remember how you were a frog once
And maybe now there are other frogs you miss

But I kissed your lips
I took the lily-pad web of your hand in mine
Until it was so much more human in design

That your fingers grew unique and fascinating prints
I could feel right there on my skin
And I laughed to see you become a prince

I took you to the castle and invited you in
Where everyone seemed to see what we did
You were the one I chose
I was the one you hid
You were the one expected
Among the secret cheaters
Rising to submit a bid
To be he who was selected the temporary king
Humpty Dumpty of the sideline
Humpty Dumpty on a fling
(That's all)
But by throwing himself into it
Realized he had just thrown himself
Off the wall

And all the queen's horses
And all the queen's men
Couldn't make him a tadpole again

## Alive in the Interior

The dreary sun over-lights the day
With its complaints
Now sharp and brilliant
Now overstated

The flowers stand where we have waited
For a message or a sign
The furious beauty of their colors cannot compete
With the soft, green pine or the shade
Or the bed of earth we left unmade

Maybe it will finally rain
Maybe we will finally see the world align
In some cosmic way
Where the night will extend itself
In ecstatic play
And reduce the angry sun
To a single, shadowed ray

I love you best in cool caves
Where we are far from the sunny, grassy graves of the dead
Instead, we are alive where there is dark, wet birth
And the sea moves in warm waves into the earth
Where the sun cannot see the sea
Or you loving me

One day we will have to move back

Out into the light

And shield our eyes

From the sight of others

As they judge us

Inferior

Because we know the secrets

Of the interior

## Elementary Season

The day is partial to itself
Even though the snow blackens into crust
At every curb
Wind chills gusting
Sidewalks spilling over
With what is left of winter's disturbing hold

The day does not care
Morning still yawns into the gray embrace of the cold
Spring is coming
And the light is getting generous and bold
The hours push back the edges of the sky
As the arctic mantle starts to fray

Will the corpse of winter finally die

I will not forget to pause
And feel winter's absence
In the beauty of the day
The way that colors creep up over what was gray
And cover every living, throbbing thing that waits
To see the winter cold relent
As flowers push their way through the cement
And every new and living thing
Will bleed laughter

As I remain afraid

Of what comes after all this life comes crawling to a stand

And winter slips itself out of the cold of my hand

To that place we all forget

Beyond ourselves

Beyond all hope, all doubt

All love and all regret


I pause in honor of December

When you were born

I stop

And I remember the white mountain

That fell around us in quiet grace

Until night came and filled the deep white space

With sleep


The moment breaks

Into the noisy shout of spring


We go outside

And leave the world we've known

The winter we have carried in our bones

Will melt away

And take us with it

Into the fragile promise of the day


We go

## The Swan's Tale

On a raw hill near Sinjar
No map of the world
Here we lived as humans
We lay down at night to stare at the stars
Told ancient stories, rode camels, drove cars
We were human enough to feel
To see, sweat, love and eat grief
Gather together in the soft feathers of our belief
As beautiful as a peacock's tail opening
In the blue air
Beautiful as a sail on the ocean

We could only dream of
Deep waters here
In the dry magnitude of a far-from-modern life
We were fathers, mothers, sisters, daughters
Sons and brothers kneeling to plumage
Until the whole village hummed with fear
And the hills turned gray
As our fate drew near
And we knew that one day soon
We would be gone

On the night before they came
I dreamt of a swan searching for its mate
On a dark lake

Full of bleached and broken human bones
Peacock feathers everywhere we used to be
Traces of families taken from their homes
But the swan only dreams this terror
And flies on
Still searching for its lost love

I dreamt of flying once
Seeing my fate from miles above these hills
Time-traveling
I could see a child running in the sunshine
With my older brother
While they were passing a ball back and forth
Unaware of all the ways a man can hate

We ran so far away
We came home dirty and late
To the dinner that sat there waiting
Made by my mother's hand
Full of a love more vast than the centuries
Of sand and suffering
That surround us now

Like the swan, I have survived somehow
An odd bird known for magic and beauty
I carry this shock
My wings cannot lift me or carry me away
From the cruelty of everything I loved

And lost in that dry lake
What that drastic morning left
In its thunderous wake

Where water used to hold us aloft
There is now a thirst
We cannot slake with human tears
As all hope of return to a better time
Disappears
Along with white vans in the fading light
Where a crisis of men and boys still fight
To kill themselves and each other

And here I am
As alone as the swan
Who opens its beak to scream
The name of its lost heart
Into the hills of Sinjar
Where it dreams nothing

# Crude Awakening

The blood of ancient creatures
Spills
From the split hull of a ship
As the water darkens, curls its lip
And a lone gull loses his way home

We swim the oily coast
And let the sun roast us gently
For a while
We bake in each other's arms
And we smile into our mortality

The birds now raise a collective alarm
As they caw over the dead fish
That pay the price
Of some dark, human wish
Of unintended harm

The genie is out of the lamp
The sand is black and damp
And sick
As the fires light
Some invisible wick of the sea
And the waters burn
Endlessly

The horizon is ice

White with sacrifice

As the smoke rises

Black and odd

From the sad altar of the sea

Rising to the sky of some modern

God of iniquity

Who will not learn our names


We cannot breathe the air

Or swim too deep

We have our own, tiny flames

To protect


As the ship bleeds

And is wrecked

## The Visit

You try to enter
Where the bark is rough-hewn
And the tree is a castle of sap
And perfume

Fairies wander the hollow trunk
Where flowers grow in fragrant bunk-beds
Where tiny heads cast dreamy spells
As wings fold in two
No one tells you the secret password
But you still know

Pay attention as you ride these dreams
You will feel the current slowly take you over
Wonderful
As the four-leaf clover that sets the table
Where you drink nectar
And live a rich fable of days

These are the stories that come to life
A thousand million ways
Each time you close your eyes
And the bluebell sprays its scent

You ask the creature what she meant
And she smiles

As if you should relent to the illusion
And smile with her at your confusion

You feel your own wings
In the rough space of skin
Growing tough between your shoulder blades
You are changing in these everglades
Where light and shadow braid together

Will you stay
Will you stay forever
Or will you break the heart of everyone
Who has gathered for your sake
You do not know if you will sleep and dream
Or you will wake

And so you climb into a tiny bunk
Of bark and flowers
For what you understand to be years or centuries
Or hours
You enter territory for which there is no map
And dream eternity
A strange and magic nap

# In the Way-Back on the Garden State

I look up to see a cathedral
Growing out of the mountain
Rising like a goddess out of a wave of stone
Dripping ivy over naked beauty
Standing out there in nature's love and cruelty
Empty, yet majestic
Ancient and alone

I used to think that mountains were tsunamis
Or at the very least volcanoes
I saw them move and change size

My brother told me one day as we drove
That the horizon was water in shock
The sunset was lava shaking
A sky of molten rock
And I trembled at the thought of it
The terrible bolt of surprise
As the disaster grew larger in my eyes
I shrank smaller into the car
Hoping the wave would not crash
That we would not be buried
In terror and ash or water and sky
I did not know exactly how it would happen
But I was fairly certain we would die

My mother could not calm me down

At night

I used to fear the monsters of the dark

She would leave on the light

But I would cower under covers

Pretending to be dead

Pretending I had faith in god

And that prayers were stronger than dread

I prayed that the monster would not

Could not

Come crawling out from under the bed


One night recently

I dreamt that my mother died

I was running into the yard

Where she lay like a child on her side

I lifted her up, and she cried

And she cried and cried

And I carried her like a doll into the house

Where everything was disrupted


And she was tiny

The size of a baby mouse

I needed to help her

I needed to save her

But she just kept getting smaller

And smaller and smaller

And forgetting the things I gave her
I kept saying her name
To keep her with me
But after a while I knew
She could not hear me call her
She could not hear me call her back

I woke up as if from an attack
I could barely breathe
From the loss
From the lack of her
From the shock of waking
From the terrible relief
Of mistaking her for someone
Fragile and dying
Someone I was trying to keep alive

Oh yes, we survive
My mother has long been dead
So long ago
There is nothing left to dread

And so I held  my dreaming waking self
The little girl who disappeared
Into a picture frame
On a shelf

I lay for a moment

And closed my eyes

I thought of a mountain

Under a lava sky

It was never water

It was a wave


It was goodbye

## Fugue State

He died of suddenness
Breath caught short in that last moment
Where everything that came before
Or could have happened after
Moved past inquiry
Or capture

He was never like the others
And as he discarded all the reasons
Excuses, stories and exchanges
Husked his spirit free of friends
Lovers, children and strangers
He forgot himself

The way we put time together
Makes it seem as if we are living in some reality
Rather than the dream of illusion and memory
We conjure along the way
All the people, names, places and feelings
We can no longer say, see, taste, touch
Or share

He is no longer here
He is no longer there
What does it mean to even mention this man
Is he still with us

With me

Still somehow a part of the divine plan


We know nothing

We pretend we understand time

And then we die

Each one of us

Submitting ourselves to the eternal suddenness

From which we emerge

And to which we shall return

## Red Sky Morning

The illusion of a wave flowing backward
Into an unnatural arc of itself
How do the waters rise
Noah did not ask
Did not wait for the surprise
Of elements to arrive

His fear is my frequent companion
I don't know how to say no
I'm afraid to stay, afraid to go
I'm afraid to go too far on the random warning—
What a beautiful morning

Are these the days that people sing about
Or are they just a crazy record
That will be played in the future
As a quaint offering of those who lived and died
A faint memory
Of another time long gone by

We look back on those waters
That drowned the world of Noah
And we smile

We dress our children as animals
We march them onto paper arks

In public parks and community productions
In ridiculous reductions of the world catastrophe

I hope you will move with me
Across the terrible waters that may come
As we leave behind the unbelieving others
Who laugh at our weird song

Follow a dark sky and wait to be wrong
Wait for the hollow moon to ride into the light again
As we hear the waters fall around us
Thick as tears
And then praise the moon when she finally appears

So now you know—
I would leave the others here to wait

But if you said no
If you said you wouldn't go
Or if you didn't seem to know
What I know
I would choose to stick around

I would stay with you, my love
And drown

## Sleight of Tongue

The first words I heard you say
Were a stutter
As if you spoke Morse code
As if you were reciting a Norse ode
Or some utter nonsense
You seemed to explode into jabberwocky

We are now watching a hockey game
With a bottle of vodka stashed in my purse
I don't know if this will get better
Or if we are headed for worse
I do know now
That you can always converse
When you want to

Alone
Like a hermit-philosopher or king
You are able to pontificate on anything
Words glisten when you speak your mind
And I try to listen
But I often find myself lost in a jumble
Where the words tumble out
All over me
And I can't think

That's why I drink

You do very badly to take refuge in mediocrity
When you are clearly not one of us
You are so much more
You are an omnibus of thought

You could say that my life has gotten caught
In a threshing machine
Like a patchwork quilt
But only halfway ripped apart
You hold me together with words
Each one a dart

My life is pictures sewn together in a dream
Flowing gently on a stream of thought
In which I start by spinning in cartwheels
And leaping from heights
Too extreme to mention

You'd say I wasn't paying attention
And that's why I fell
I'd say it's because I heard you speaking
Strange tongues
As you wove a magic spell
And I knew I had to learn that code
To speak that language
To understand the story you told

A dream is forgotten
Because it has to be forgotten
Or we cannot go on
Found in fragments
We make something whole of it
We make sense of what is gone
Or arriving
We build a context for surviving

The whole thing is so sad
For some unknown reason
Like blossoms bursting forth
Full of faith
In the wrong season
(Is the weather really strange
Or just a fever-chill of climate change)

Old voices still stutter inside me
Fragments of a story I found
In pieces of paper left on the ground

You'd say you love me
And you'd smooth away my fears
We will make something new
You'd say
When the old world disappears

## Harvesting Shadows

We looked for the light everywhere
Except where it was
I could not see the darkness
In the darkness
I could not see that it held what I was seeking
What it held was permanent
And yet blinking between versions of itself
The truth, for me, was melding
With a wealth of misunderstandings

But you are the kind of person
Who likes to plan things

I held your hand
And that too was a form of darkness between us
I could feel you, and I knew
That somewhere
Perhaps someone had seen us

You were the light I found inside
You were where the darkness opened
Wide and true
Where I did not have to see anything
I could just feel
And know it was you

This is the place
We have been harvesting shadows
Fruit of life from the dark tree
The roots are where we draw our strength
The sky is where we reach to be

Who knew
That it is only by reaching down
That we emerge
It is where the hot molten creative center
Starts to surge
To rise into the scalding fountain
That will cool one day
Into an ancient mountain
Full of trees

I hold your hand
And—*carpe diem*
We are what we seize
Let's grab the day
And hold it between us
In an ordinary way

I will hold the rose
I will feel the thorn
Right there where the skin is torn
In order to have the flower

I will hold your hand

For this day

This moment

This hour

Whatever we are given

I will know it's right


And in the darkness I cannot see

I will still feel the light

## Earlier in the Day

The poem sits like a worm
Excited at both ends
Wanting to connect with itself
Or something like itself

The poem waits for the word to uncurl
To slither in the earth fearlessly
The worm has no idea it is ugly
It is a beautiful thing

This poem lacks the grace of the worm
These words are not what they want to be
They want to be flying
In a royal flock
They want to lead the other words
In a parade of stars
And feathers
To be loved for better and for worse
To sing in a perfect key
Unlocking the secrets of the universe
Singing the song of the galaxies they traverse
The ultimate verse
And to sing that song of origin
Multiverses and the choruses too
That's what the words want to do

The worm does not care about that

Does not care if the earth is curved or flat

The worm is unaware of the atmosphere

Lifting its skirt to let the sun rise

The worm is in the dirt

Wiggling with joy and surprise

The worm is love


And the words that fly above

Look down with hunger

With desire

On that rich squirming life

And meat


And as they come down

They forget

You are what you eat


And now

The worm

And the bird

Are somehow

Complete

# *Doubts*

Do not let them in
They eat dreams
Color first
But they eat everything
Including the skin
Do not let them play
They always win

Doubts get fat on what you fear
To love
They are always right there
Beside you
Or sometimes hovering above

Doubts love whispering
In your own voice
Into your secret ear
Doubts linger even when
They pretend to go away
Even so, they are still near

Doubts will not ever be
Your friend
They will seduce you
They will lie to you
They will allow you to imagine

And pretend
Whatever is untrue

Doubts live forever
Doubts never end

When a doubt offers you a gloved hand
You must say no
You must not try to understand
Or to explain
You must not argue
You must not blame
You must continue to be the same
Or better than you were

Doubts are insidious
Wherever they occur
They stay stuck in your emotions
Doubts pretend
They are an ocean
And they invite you to drown
You must hold a doubt down
Until it stops breathing
If a doubt comes back
Make it write you a letter
Full of its seething, broken teeth
And its false attack

When you see a doubt
Turn your back on it
Or if you must
Come right up to it
Break its trust
And stare it in the face
Tell a doubt you don't believe it
You will not draw it into being
In fact
You will erase its sneering face
Until it is a mere smudge

Sometimes
When a doubt is strong
You will be tempted
To budge in its direction
To play along
To sing its song

Don't ever play
Doubts will always betray
Instead
Conduct an orchestra of belief
In your head
Let every instrument sing praise
Until you raise the horizon
And turn a doubt into a pale wraith
That fades from view

Court faith, court beauty, court gratitude

And express your happiness

In thunderous different ways


When your world goes broken

And you have too much room for doubts

Remember this:

Tell doubts to get out

And instead

Invite yourself to receive joy


Invite yourself

To perceive what is possible

To what you believe

To what you hope

To what you know

And can see to be real


Doubts will steal and eat your dreams

But only if you let them

The best way to defeat them

Is to leave them

And forget them

## Resist Allow

Gorging on the sky
I am bloated and delirious
With beauty
There are no words
For the dance of the sea
Or the flight of white birds
That beat their wings
Where my heart should be

You are always there
Where I am most alive
On this too perfect coast

The ocean gives itself to me
Too large to hold
Or even see
With common eyes

You are what my heart denies
You are the most beautiful places
I fear
And the deepest embraces
Of surprise
Where I am clear
For once
And always

There is too much beauty
For me to feel
To touch
To taste

But I still try

Life runs so deep
And wide
And with such haste
There is no time
To waste

I fill my lungs until they ache
I breathe myself
And then I face
The beauty that surrounds me
Now

Resist
Allow
Resist
Allow

## Julie Flanders

**Julie Flanders** is known for her passionate and haunting texts.

With deceptively simple words, she guides readers through the mysteries of the familiar to a deeper understanding of life and love, death and loss, miracles of perception and the magic of the ordinary.

An award-winning songwriter, her musical use of language is well known to the many fans of **October Project**, a band she co-founded with composer Emil Adler and for which she writes all the lyrics.

She is also an acclaimed creative success coach and hypnotherapist whose clients have included Academy Award winners, *New York Times* best-selling authors, performers and creative entrepreneurs in all walks of life.

*julieflanderspoetry.com | julieflanders.com | octoberprojectmusic.com*

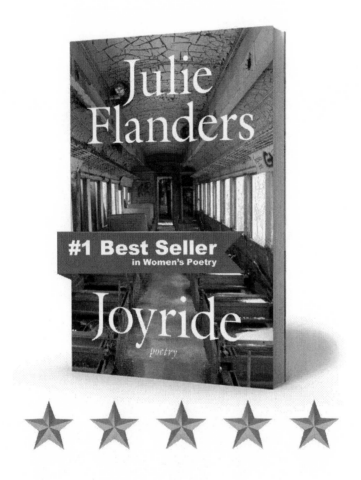

**octoberprojectmusic.com**

Made in the USA
Columbia, SC
04 December 2019